Great African Americans
Politics

By Steve Goldsworthy

www.av2books.com

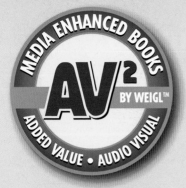

AV² provides enriched content that supplements and complements this book. Weigl's AV² books strive to create inspired learning and engage young minds in a total learning experience.

Your AV² Media Enhanced books come alive with...

Audio
Listen to sections of the book read aloud.

Key Words
Study vocabulary, and complete a matching word activity.

Video
Watch informative video clips.

Quizzes
Test your knowledge.

Go to www.av2books.com, and enter this book's unique code.

Embedded Weblinks
Gain additional information for research.

Slide Show
View images and captions, and prepare a presentation.

BOOK CODE

F369260

Try This!
Complete activities and hands-on experiments.

... and much, much more!

AV² by Weigl brings you media enhanced books that support active learning.

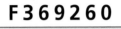

Published by AV² by Weigl
350 5th Avenue, 59th Floor
New York, NY 10118

Website: www.av2books.com   www.weigl.com
Copyright ©2012 AV2 by Weigl

Library of Congress Cataloging-in-Publication Data

Goldsworthy, Steve.
 Politics : African American history / Steve Goldsworthy.
    p. cm. -- (Great African Americans)
 Includes bibliographical references and index.
 ISBN 978-1-61690-662-7 (hardcover : alk. paper) -- ISBN 978-1-61690-666-5 (softcover : alk. paper)
 1. African Americans--Politics and government--Juvenile literature. 2. African Americans--History--Juvenile literature. 3. African Americans--Civil rights--History--Juvenile literature. I. Title.
 E185.6.G65 2012
 973'.0496073--dc22
                              2010050182

Printed in the United States of America in North Mankato, Minnesota
1 2 3 4 5 6 7 8 9 0 15 14 13 12 11

062011
WEP290411

Weigl acknowledges Getty Images as its primary image supplier for this title.

Every reasonable effort has been made to trace ownership and to obtain permission to reprint copyright material. The publishers would be pleased to have any errors or omissions brought to their attention so that they may be corrected in subsequent printings.

Senior Editor: Heather Kissock
Art Director: Terry Paulhus

Contents

GREAT AFRICAN AMERICANS

A Great Journey

African American history, with its struggles for freedom and **civil rights**, is filled with tragedy and victory. Politics has always played a role in African American history. There have been African American politicians in the United States for hundreds of years. Many important advances in civil rights have come as a result of the efforts of African American political leaders.

This great journey has spanned almost 400 years. The journey began when the first slave ships arrived in America in the early 1600s and continues through the swearing in of the nation's first African American president, Barack Obama, in 2009.

African Americans were involved in politics long before the American colonies declared independence from Great Britain in 1776. The first African American elected to a **legislative** body may have been Mathias de Sousa. In 1638, de Sousa, the servant of a Catholic priest, arrived in what is now Maryland. He earned his freedom and eventually entered politics. He was elected to the Maryland General Assembly in 1641. Sadly, he served only one year before being forced back to work to pay off debts.

Historic Case

Born in about 1795, Dred Scott was a slave owned by a doctor in Missouri. His owner took him to Illinois, where slavery was illegal. After his return to the South, Scott sued for his freedom, claiming that his time in Illinois had made him free. His case went all the way to the **U.S. Supreme Court**. In a controversial 1857 decision, the Court ruled that African Americans, free or enslaved, were not considered U.S. **citizens**. Therefore, Scott's case was dismissed.

Early Political Figures

Harriet Tubman was a famous figure before and during the **Civil War**. Born into slavery in Maryland in 1820, Tubman was treated cruelly by her owners. After years of abuse, she escaped in 1849.

Tubman was determined to free others, including her own family. She used a secret network of hideouts and safe houses known as the **Underground Railroad**. Tubman led hundreds of escaped slaves from the South to freedom in northern states or in Canada.

During the Civil War, Tubman served as a scout and spy for the Union forces. She even helped plan a raid in South Carolina that freed 750 slaves in 1863. Harriet Tubman was buried with military honors in 1913.

First African American Senator
The first African American to serve in the U.S. Senate was Hiram Rhodes

On the Underground Railroad, Harriet Tubman served as a guide, or "conductor." Escaping slaves were called "passengers."

A U.S. Representative

Robert Smalls, born a slave in 1839 in South Carolina, was forced to serve in the Confederate army during the Civil War. In 1861, he and several other slaves took control of a Confederate ship and surrendered it to the Union fleet. It was a brave and daring feat.

After the war, Smalls bought his former owner's estate. He became a successful businessman and a member of the South Carolina state legislature. In 1875, Smalls was elected to the U.S. House of Representatives. He was also one of the founders of the **Republican Party** of South Carolina.

In the 1870s, Hiram Rhodes Revels headed a school for African Americans in Mississippi now called Alcorn State University.

Revels. He was born in 1827 to free parents in North Carolina. Revels was never a slave. He entered politics in Natchez, Mississippi, during **Reconstruction**. After serving in the Mississippi State Senate, he was elected to the U.S. Senate in 1870. A remarkable speaker, Revels worked to improve the rights of African American workers.

The War Between the States

During the Civil War, Northern states battled the Southern states that had seceded, or left, the Union. The Confederate army fought for the 11 Southern states that seceded. The Union army was the armed forces for the U.S. **federal** government. A major issue in the war, which lasted from 1861 to 1865, was slavery.

TECHNOLOGY LINK

To learn more about the Underground Railroad, visit **www.nationalgeographic. com/railroad.**

Frederick Douglass

Writer, public speaker, and statesman Frederick Douglass was born a slave named Frederick Augustus Washington Bailey in 1817 in Maryland. As a young boy, he worked as a house servant in Baltimore. Although it was illegal to teach slaves to read, his owner's wife taught young Frederick the alphabet. Frederick Douglass began to teach himself to read and write in secret. "Knowledge," he later said, "is the pathway from slavery to freedom."

A New Start

After several attempts, Frederick Douglass escaped slavery in 1838, disguised as a sailor. He traveled to New York City and later to Massachusetts. He attended meetings of antislavery groups, including the Bristol Anti-Slavery Society. He was an intelligent and expressive speaker.

At age 23, Frederick Douglass gave his first speech to the Massachusetts Anti-Slavery Society. He moved the crowd with his powerful description of life as a slave. In 1845, he published an autobiography called *Narrative of the Life of Frederick Douglass, an American Slave*. The well-received book established him as a leader of the movement against slavery in the United States.

The Civil War and After

The outbreak of the Civil War in 1861 brought slavery to the forefront of American politics. Frederick Douglass continued to work tirelessly for African American rights. He served as an important adviser to President Abraham Lincoln during this time.

On January 1, 1863, Lincoln issued the **Emancipation Proclamation**. It declared all slaves free in areas of the South controlled by the Confederacy. In 1865, the 13th **Amendment** to the U.S. Constitution ended slavery throughout the United States.

In 1872, a supporter of women's rights named Victoria Woodhull ran for president with Frederick Douglass as her running mate. They did not win. Douglass served in other public offices, including as a U.S. marshal in 1881. For the rest of his life, he lectured about voting rights for African Americans and women. Douglass died in 1895.

Although it did not free all enslaved people in the country, the Emancipation Proclamation was a great achievement for the Lincoln administration.

Booker T. Washington

One of history's most influential African American political leaders was Booker T. Washington. Booker Taliaferro Washington was born in 1856 in Hale's Ford, Virginia. His mother was a slave. He knew very little about his father, who was of European ancestry.

Freedom

One day, when Booker was about nine years old, a stranger came to their owner's house. He made a speech, rolled out a large piece of paper, and read it to all the slaves. It was the Emancipation Proclamation, which had been issued in 1863. Booker and his young brother and sister did not know what it meant. When the man left, Booker's mother turned to her children with tears in her eyes. It was 1865. The Civil War had ended, and Booker T. Washington and his family had been declared free.

Booker T. Washington attended school and also worked in a coal mine and a salt furnace to help support his family. He later went to Hampton Normal and Agricultural Institute in Virginia and Wayland Seminary in Washington, D.C. Then, Washington returned to Hampton Institute to teach. The ambitious 25-year-old was offered the chance to lead a similar school in Alabama. On July 4, 1881, the Tuskegee Normal and Industrial Institute was founded with Washington as its principal.

Washington inspired his African American students to build their own school. They constructed classrooms and barns, planted and tended crops, and raised livestock. Washington stressed learning a trade such as carpentry or construction, as well as academic skills such as writing and mathematics. He believed that effort and education would gain African Americans the respect and acceptance of other Americans. The school he led grew to become the well-regarded Tuskegee University.

Booker T. Washington gave many stirring speeches during his life. He spoke to audiences about how to improve social and economic conditions for African Americans.

Another View

Washington had his critics. They supported full rights for African Americans immediately. Washington continued to emphasize the importance of African American hard work and ingenuity. He believed this approach would lead eventually to more equal treatment of African Americans in American society. Booker T. Washington's dedication to improving the lives of African Americans laid the groundwork for the civil rights movement of the 1950s and 1960s.

Quick Facts

Booker took the last name Washington after entering school at age nine. Only at school did he realize that the other children had last names. Later, when he discovered his mother had given him Taliaferro for a last name at birth, he used it as a middle name.

In 1901, Booker T. Washington was served dinner at the White House with President Theodore Roosevelt. He was the first African American invited to dine at the White House.

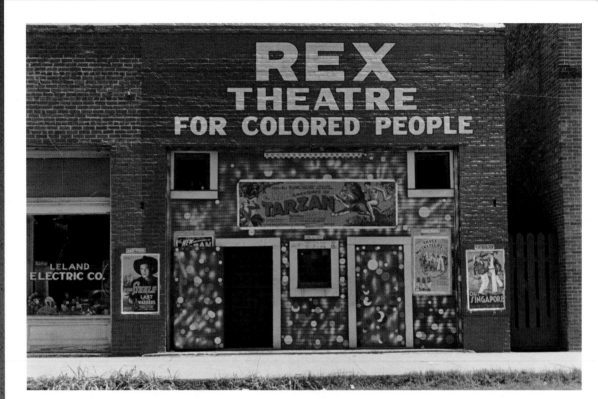

"Separate but Equal"

Jim Crow laws generally refer to local and state laws for racial segregation. They were enacted mainly in southern states in the late 1800s and early 1900s. These laws technically gave African Americans a "separate but equal" status in the United States. African Americans existed separately but, in reality, rarely equally under these laws. The term *Jim Crow laws* comes from a **racist** show routine from the 1820s that featured an African American character named Jim Crow.

Soon after the period known as Reconstruction ended in the South in 1877, new political leaders gained control of state and local governments there. These leaders introduced so-called Jim Crow laws to satisfy some of their racist supporters. In addition, governments in the South placed limits and rules on anyone who wanted to vote. They required citizens to pass reading tests and pay a tax before they could vote. These measures made it difficult for many African Americans to take part in the political process.

Separation by Law
Jim Crow laws were passed in southern states that required separate public schools for African

Americans. African Americans also had to use separate bathrooms, restaurants, parks, drinking fountains, and seating areas on public transportation. The public places, buildings, and services for African Americans were usually below the quality offered to others.

The U.S. **Congress** passed the Civil Rights Act in 1875, guaranteeing equal rights to African Americans. However, segregation continued. In fact, the Supreme Court declared the act **unconstitutional** in 1883.

Court Challenges

Many people protested these unjust laws. One African American named Homer Plessy was arrested in Louisiana for sitting in a train car reserved for people of European ancestry. He fought the arrest in the courts. Plessy took his case all the way to the Supreme Court, but he lost. The 1896 *Plessy v. Ferguson* decision said that it was legal to have "separate but equal" public places for different races. This ruling would stand for more than 50 years.

Quick Facts

Some of the first Jim Crow laws in the South involved separation of the races on public transportation. These laws segregated African Americans and people of European ancestry in railway cars.

Jim Crow laws forbid marriage between an African American and a person of European descent.

Laws of racial segregation separated African Americans from the rest of society in hospitals, in movie theaters, in cemeteries, and on the baseball fields. There were even segregated performances of the circus.

An Organization for Political Change

The National Association for the Advancement of Colored People, or NAACP, is the oldest and largest civil rights organization in the United States. The term *colored* is no longer used to refer to African Americans, though it has historical significance. Founded in 1909, the NAACP remains one of the strongest institutions for political change in the United States. Its headquarters is located in Baltimore, Maryland.

The goal of the NAACP is to secure "political, educational, social, and economic equality of rights of all persons and to eliminate racial hatred and racial **discrimination**." The organization advances its goal through the court system, political action, and educational programs. The NAACP fights racial discrimination in the workplace, voting booths, housing, and schools. It also celebrates the achievements of people of color with various awards.

Du Bois and the Niagara Movement

W. E. B. Du Bois was a scholar and civil rights **activist**. In 1895, he became the first African American to earn a **doctorate degree** from Harvard University. Unlike

W. E. B. Du Bois wrote more than 20 books, including *The Souls of Black Folk* in 1903, which called for equality for African Americans.

Booker T. Washington, Du Bois did not believe in gradual gains in African American rights. He believed African Americans deserved the same rights as anyone else. He had no intention of waiting for anything.

In 1905, some African American leaders met near Niagara Falls to form the Niagara Movement. The group had planned to meet on the U.S. side of Niagara Falls. Unable to find hotel rooms for

African Americans there, they went to Canada. At the meeting, the group, led by Du Bois, demanded an end to racial discrimination.

Founding the NAACP

In 1908, a deadly **race riot** broke out in Springfield, Illinois. Angered by a crime supposedly committed by an African American man, mobs took to the streets. They hanged two African Americans and burned homes and businesses. Thousands of African Americans fled the city in fear.

Shocked and outraged leaders of different races met after the riots. Their meetings resulted in the formation of the NAACP. Among its 60 founders were Niagara Movement members Du Bois, Mary Church Terrell, and Ida B. Wells-Barnett.

A reporter and former teacher, Wells-Barnett was a powerful advocate for the rights of African Americans and women. In 1884 in Ohio, she refused to move to a "colored" railroad car and was forced to leave the train. She sued the railroad company, bringing attention to the racial inequalities of her time.

Mary Church Terrell studied classical literature at Oberlin College in Ohio. A school principal, she became the first African American to serve on the Board of Education in Washington, D.C. Together, these

Mary Church Terrell was born in 1863 to former slaves in Memphis, Tennessee.

people and many others helped shape the objectives and vision of today's NAACP.

A Legal Leader

Thurgood Marshall played an important role in the NAACP. Born Thoroughgood Marshall in Baltimore, Maryland, in 1908, he had a great-grandfather who was an African-born slave. Thurgood's parents raised him to respect the law and fight for the defenseless. After graduating from Frederick Douglass High School in 1925, Thurgood Marshall tried to study law at the University of Maryland but was refused admittance because of his race.

Becoming a Lawyer

Marshall attended Howard University School of Law. He graduated first in his class in 1933. Then, Marshall set up his own law practice and began working with the NAACP.

Marshall's first major success took place in 1936. He sued the University of Maryland, the same school that barred him from entering, on behalf of another African American student and won. Marshall went on to win many civil rights cases for African Americans, including his first Supreme Court case in 1940. That same year, he became chief counsel for the NAACP. He argued more than 30 cases before the Supreme Court.

Marshall's most famous Supreme Court case was *Brown v. Board of Education*. In 1954, Marshall disputed the claim that two separate public schools for two different races was constitutional. He argued that the African American school system was not equal, and in fact, greatly inferior.

The Supreme Court agreed, overturning the 1896 *Plessy v. Ferguson* decision. The historic ruling declared segregation in public schools unconstitutional. African Americans now had the right to attend the same public schools as people of European descent. Marshall's win paved the way for the end of legal segregation in the United States.

Becoming a Justice

In 1961, President John F. Kennedy named Thurgood Marshall to be a judge on the U.S. Court of Appeals. President Johnson appointed him the first African American solicitor general in 1965. The solicitor general is the person who represents the government in the Supreme Court. In 1967, Johnson named Marshall the first African American Supreme Court justice.

The Browns sued the Board of Education of Topeka, Kansas, for the right to send their daughter Linda to a nearby "white" school.

He Had a Dream

No African American leader had more of an impact on U.S. politics than Dr. Martin Luther King Jr. Pastor, civil rights activist, and gifted public speaker, King was a legendary voice for social change. King was born in Atlanta, Georgia, on January 15, 1929. He attended Booker T. Washington High School. An exceptionally bright student, he was accepted to Morehouse College at age 15. He studied religion and earned a doctorate degree at Boston University in 1955. In 1954, at age 25, King became a pastor in Montgomery, Alabama.

In 1955, King was inspired by the story of a woman named Rosa Parks, who refused to move to a "colored" section of a Montgomery city bus. Soon after, King led the Montgomery Bus **Boycott,** in which African Americans refused to ride city buses. The peaceful protest lasted for more than a year. Although King was arrested, the boycott ended racial segregation on all city buses in Montgomery.

After Montgomery
After the success in Montgomery, King formed the Southern Christian Leadership Conference, or SCLC, in

1957. The goal of the organization was equality for African Americans through nonviolent protest. The SCLC became one of the country's main civil rights groups.

In 1959, King visited the birthplace of Indian leader Mahatma Gandhi. Gandhi had long been a powerful influence on the civil rights leader. Gandhi's belief in nonviolent protest to achieve political goals moved and inspired King to continue his work.

King faced many opponents during his life. Through the years, he endured insults and arrests. His enemies threw rocks at him, threatened his family, and bombed his home. King was determined to work for peaceful political change, however.

In the 1960s, King pressured the U.S. government to end the Vietnam War. He believed the country should focus on helping the poor and unemployed in the United States. Many politicians, including President Johnson, disagreed with King about Vietnam.

Tragedy

On April 4, 1968, Martin Luther King Jr. was shot dead at a motel during a trip to Memphis, Tennessee. He had been there to support the rights of African American workers. The world grieved at his death, but the tragedy inspired followers to continue working toward King's vision of equality for all Americans.

Famous Words

On August 28, 1963, King participated in the peaceful political rally called the March on Washington. It was here, on the steps of the Lincoln Memorial in Washington, D.C., that King made his best-known speech. "I have a dream," he said, "that my four little children will one day live in a nation where they will not be judged by the color of their skin but by the content of their character."

The Civil Rights Movement

Led by Martin Luther King Jr., the civil rights movement was an organized effort to win racial equality for all Americans. The civil rights movement was famous for its nonviolent protests known as civil disobedience. Protests included peaceful marches, group prayers and song at sites of civil injustice, and **sit-ins**. The legal system and the historic *Brown v. Board of Education* ruling also played a part in political change.

Little Rock

After the 1954 *Brown v. Board of Education* decision, towns and cities in the South were forced to integrate their public schools. They took their time, however. In 1957, Little Rock, the capital of Arkansas, experienced a crisis over integration.

Nine African American students had successfully sued the state for the right to attend the newly integrated Little Rock Central High School. Orval Faubus, the governor of Arkansas, was not in favor of integration. He intended to block the students from attending the school. U.S. troops had to be called in to protect the children at school.

Sit-ins and Freedom Riders

In 1960, four African American students staged a sit-in at a Woolworth's in Greensboro, North Carolina. The students sat down at the segregated lunch counter. After being refused service, they remained in their seats to protest the store's unfair policies. The event won much attention and inspired sit-ins at

In 1957, U.S. soldiers escorted African American students into the segregated high school in Little Rock, Arkansas.

libraries, beaches, movie theaters, museums, and parks throughout the South.

Civil rights workers began traveling on buses through the South. During their travel, they tested new laws that made segregation for interstate travel illegal. These people were called Freedom Riders.

The Congress of Racial Equality, or CORE, which was founded in 1942 in Chicago, Illinois, organized the first Freedom Ride on May 2, 1961. Activists rode a bus from Washington, D.C., to New Orleans, Louisiana. They stopped along the way to use desegregated restrooms, water fountains, lunch counters, and bus terminals. Although some opponents attacked and beat them, activists found the courage to assert their rights.

An Important Victory

After years of political protest and sacrifice, civil rights activists had a significant victory. The Civil Rights Act of 1964, which outlawed discrimination based on gender, race, color, religion, or national origin, was signed into law. Racial segregation in the United States was illegal.

President Lyndon B. Johnson signed the Civil Rights Act of 1964 in Washington, D.C., before shaking the hand of civil rights leader Martin Luther King Jr.

Quick Facts

Rosa Parks is sometimes called "the mother of the civil rights movement" for refusing to give up her seat on a public bus in 1954. Her act was nonviolent, but it sparked a powerful protest and led to significant change.

Martin Luther King Jr. was jailed several times for his acts of nonviolent civil disobedience. He wrote a famous political paper from jail. Written in the margins of a newspaper, it is known as "Letter from a Birmingham Jail."

African American political activists adopted a jail-no-**bail** policy. When arrested, they chose to serve in prison rather than pay a fine. They did not support giving money to a legal system that did not honor their civil rights.

Malcolm X

One controversial figure during the civil rights movement was a man who called himself Malcolm X. He was a radical activist. Malcolm X believed in securing African American freedom, justice, and equality "by any means necessary."

Early Years

Malcolm Little was born in Omaha, Nebraska, in 1925. His father was a Baptist minister and activist who raised Malcolm and his brothers and sisters to be proud of who they were. The **terrorist** group known as the **Ku Klux Klan** harassed the Little family, however.

Although Malcolm was an excellent student, a teacher told him that his wish to become a lawyer was a foolish dream for an African American. He later settled in the New York City neighborhood of Harlem, where he fell into a life of crime. In 1946, Malcolm was arrested for robbery and sentenced to ten years in prison.

Nation of Islam

In prison, Malcolm X converted to the religion of **Islam**. He discovered the Nation of Islam. This was a religious organization that preached about African American pride and self-reliance.

Malcolm Little had a difficult childhood. By the time Malcolm was 13, his father had died and his mother was in a mental institution.

Malcolm left prison in 1952. He met with Elijah Muhammad, the leader of the Nation of Islam. At this time, Malcolm changed his last name to X. It was a rejection of the practice of slave owners giving their slaves their family names.

Malcolm X soon became a powerful and persuasive speaker in the Nation of Islam. He told his followers that African Americans were superior to others. While others fought against racial segregation, Malcolm X supported separation of the races. He even believed that African Americans should have their own country. Although his ideas were radical, they often reflected growing frustration for many African Americans.

New Direction

Malcolm X's outspoken style created tensions within the Nation of Islam. Finally, in 1964, Malcolm X left the group. He founded the Organization of Afro-American Unity, or OAAU.

Malcolm X traveled to Mecca, a holy site for Muslims in Saudi Arabia. He also traveled to Africa, France, and the United Kingdom. As a result of his travels, Malcolm X came to realize that racial segregation of any kind was wrong.

When he returned to the United States, Malcolm X began receiving death threats. The threats came from

Quick Facts

Malcolm X influenced many people, including heavyweight boxer Cassius Clay. The boxer later converted to Islam and changed his name to Muhammad Ali.

Malcolm X co-wrote *The Autobiography of Malcolm X* with journalist Alex Haley between 1963 and 1965. It was one of the century's most influential books.

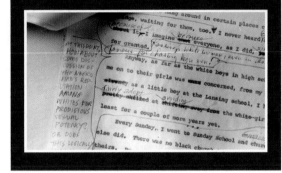

members of the Nation of Islam. On February 21, 1965, Malcolm X was shot and killed in New York by three men of the Nation of Islam.

Malcolm X spoke for many angry African Americans in the 1950s and 1960s.

Political Unrest of the 1960s

The 1960s were a time of great political gains for African Americans. However, it was also a time of political unrest. Many cities, and many African American residents in those cities, were struggling economically, and tensions sometimes ran high.

Riots and Aftermath

On July 16, 1964, in Harlem, New York, a police officer of European ancestry shot a 15-year-old African American. Although the officer said the boy had threatened him with a knife, the next day it was revealed that the boy had had no weapon.

African Americans took to the streets in protest. Residents burned and looted businesses not run by African Americans. Similar riots took place in Brooklyn, New York, and later in Philadelphia, Pennsylvania.

The federal government tried to help by passing laws intended to provide jobs and training for young African Americans. However, conditions did not improve quickly in poor inner-city neighborhoods. In 1965, a riot broke out in the South Central Los Angeles neighborhood of Watts after police officers arrested a young African American man for drunk driving. The six-day riot resulted in the deaths of 34 people and damage totaling $30 million.

President Johnson created the National Advisory Commission on Civil Disorder in 1967. The goal of the commission was to "investigate the origins of the recent disorders in [the] cities." The commission's findings led to improvements in education, employment, and social welfare for African Americans.

Black Power

In 1966, activist Stokely Carmichael, leader of the Student Nonviolent Coordinating Committee, or SNCC, began using the term *Black Power*. Against the principles of his organization, he urged African Americans to arm themselves if necessary against groups such as the Ku Klux Klan.

The idea of Black Power even found its way into sports. During the 1968 Summer Olympics in Mexico City, two African American athletes lifted a black-gloved hand in a Black Power salute during their medal ceremony. Although many people considered the act controversial, it won worldwide attention for the African American struggle for political power.

Tommie Smith and John Carlos won gold and bronze medals respectively in the 200-meter dash at the 1968 Olympics.

SNCC

Originally a student-run group, the Student Nonviolent Coordinating Committee was founded in 1960. Its goal was civil rights for African Americans. SNCC organized sit-ins and voter enrollment drives in the South. With Stokely Carmichael as its leader, the group turned more radical. SNCC had disbanded by the early 1970s.

MR. BROOKE
MASSACHUSETTS

A Shining Example: Edward Brooke

During the civil unrest of the 1960s, Edward Brooke was a shining example of what an African American politician could achieve with dedication and hard work. Born in 1919, in Washington, D.C., Edward Brooke was a conscientious student. He graduated from the all–African American Howard University in 1941. When **World War II** broke out, he went to Europe to fight with the segregated 366th **Infantry** Regiment of the U.S. Army. Brooke served for five years. He then earned a law degree from Boston University in 1948.

A Political Life

Two years after graduating, Brooke decided to go into politics. He campaigned for a seat in the Massachusetts House of Representatives. Although he lost, he gained valuable lessons about the political process.

In 1962, Brooke was elected attorney general of Massachusetts. No other African American in any state had ever been elected attorney general. Brooke soon gained a reputation for being tough on crime, especially organized crime.

In 1966, Brooke again made history. He became the state's first African American to be elected by popular vote to the U.S. Senate. President Johnson immediately appointed him to the Commission on Civil Disorders, the group organized to investigate the race riots of the 1960s.

In 1968, Brooke coauthored the 1968 Fair Housing Act, which forbids the refusal to sell or rent housing to anyone based on race, color, religion, or national origin. During the early 1970s, Brooke continued to be a political voice for education, labor issues, and human rights. He spoke out against government corruption.

Honors

After leaving the U.S. Senate in 1979, Brooke continued to practice law. He also continued to fight for low income housing and civil rights. President George W. Bush awarded Brooke the Presidential Medal of Freedom in 2004. This is the highest civilian award granted by the U.S. government. Brooke also received the Congressional Gold Medal from President Barack Obama in 2009.

Panthers and Politicians of the 1970s

If the 1960s was a time of political unrest for African Americans, the 1970s was a period of political revolution. Many African Americans felt pride in their history. They enjoyed the freedom and respect the civil rights movement had worked so hard to achieve. Others were not satisfied, however.

Black Panthers

Huey Newton and Bobby Seale founded the Black Panther Party in 1966 in Oakland, California. Influenced by the ideas of Malcolm X, they sought to stop racial inequality "by any means necessary."

Dressed in black leather jackets and sometimes armed, they fought back against police brutality in African American neighborhoods. The Black Panthers also organized clothing and food distribution programs for poor people, self-defense classes, and free medical clinics. They helped to promote pride in African American culture. Their violent actions often overshadowed these efforts, however.

Finally, after many deadly clashes with police, the party was

At its peak, the Black Panther Party had as many as 2,000 members.

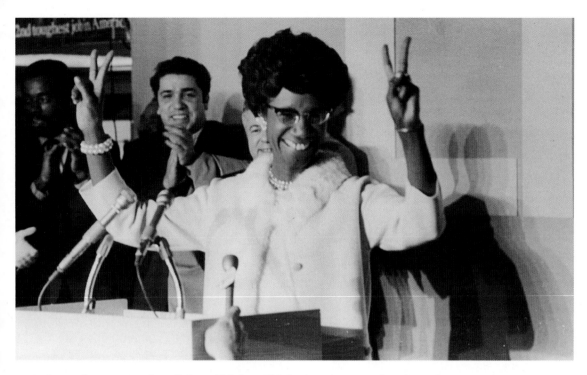

Before she entered politics, Shirley Chisholm was a schoolteacher.

disbanded in 1976. Many of its former members joined various levels of government. Others never forgot their revolutionary roots.

Politicians

Meanwhile, in traditional politics, African Americans were winning elective office. In 1968, Shirley Chisholm became the first African American woman to be elected to the U.S. Congress. Representing a district in Brooklyn, New York, she served seven terms. She hired many women and African Americans to work in her office. In 1972, Chisholm ran for the presidential nomination of the **Democratic Party**.

There were many other African Americans serving in the U.S. Congress in the 1970s, including Andrew Young of Georgia. Young, who worked for the SCLC in the 1960s, was a member of the U.S. Congress from 1973 to 1977. Then, President Jimmy Carter appointed him ambassador to the United Nations. Young was the first African American to hold that position.

On the local level, the country's first African American mayor took office in the 1970s. In 1973, Thomas Bradley became the first African American mayor of Los Angeles, California. He served for 20 years, overseeing great economic growth for the city.

Jesse Jackson

For many decades, Jesse Jackson has been a dynamic leader in U.S. politics. He was most prominent in the 1980s. Born Jesse Louis Burns in 1941, in Greenville, South Carolina, he later took his stepfather's last name. Jesse was a good student and baseball player.

After attending the University of Illinois in 1959, Jackson graduated from a college in North Carolina. He studied at the Chicago Theological Seminary but dropped out to join the civil rights movement. Later, in 1968, Jackson became a minister.

Part of the Movement
In 1966, Martin Luther King Jr. appointed Jackson to head Operation Breadbasket. This arm of the SCLC was dedicated to improving economic conditions for African Americans. Over the next several years, Jackson organized boycotts of businesses that discriminated against African Americans. He also led other nonviolent civil rights protests.

After months of disagreement with SCLC leaders, Jackson resigned from the group and formed Operation PUSH, or People United to Save Humanity. This new group focused on civil rights, social justice, and political activism. The group supported better schools for inner-city youth and provided help with job placement. As the group grew, so did its political influence.

Presidential Politics and Beyond
In 1984, Jackson ran for the Democratic presidential nomination. He became the first African American to win significant support. During his campaign, Jackson called his core of supporters the Rainbow Coalition. This coalition became a political organization that worked for the political empowerment of all people.

In 1988, Jackson again ran for the Democratic nomination for U.S. president. Despite winning some states, he was defeated by Michael Dukakis, governor of Massachusetts, who lost to George H. W. Bush in the general election.

In 1996, PUSH and the Rainbow Coalition merged. Jackson is president of Rainbow/PUSH, which works to "protect, defend, and gain civil rights" and "promote peace and justice around the world."

TECHNOLOGY LINK
To learn more about the Reverend Jesse Jackson, visit his radio website at
http://keephopealiveradio.com.

Political Gains of the 1980s and 1990s

African Americans continued their political gains in the 1980s and 1990s. During this time, the country saw its first African Americans in a variety of political roles. For example, Douglas Wilder, the grandson of slaves, won the governorship of Virginia in 1989. He was the country's first African American governor.

Douglas Wilder was the first African American member of the state senate in Virginia in the twentieth century.

Carol Moseley Braun worked as a lawyer before she ran for political office.

Clarence Thomas, next to his wife, Virginia, was sworn in by Justice Byron White in 1991. President George H. W. Bush and wife Barbara were also present.

Political Leaders

The first African American woman elected to the U.S. Senate was Carol Moseley Braun. She was sworn in as a U.S. senator for the state of Illinois in 1993. Moseley Braun was first elected to public office in 1978 as a member of the Illinois House of Representatives. She supported civil rights and education. Moseley Braun was only the second African American to serve in the U.S. Senate in the twentieth century, after Edward Brooke of Massachusetts.

The first African American to head a major political party was Ronald H. Brown. In 1989, Brown was elected chair of the Democratic National Committee. He also became the first African American secretary of commerce in 1993.

With the 1990s came the first female African American to lead a major city. In 1991, Sharon Pratt Kelly took office as the mayor of Washington, D.C. She was also the city's first female mayor.

Judicial Leader

African American judges also made gains during this time. In 1991, Clarence Thomas, of Pin Point, Georgia, became the second African American to serve on the Supreme Court, replacing retiring justice Thurgood Marshall. President George H. W. Bush appointed Thomas to the nation's highest court.

A Quiet Leader

Statesman and retired four-star general Colin Powell has been one of the great African American leaders of his time. Colin Luther Powell was born in 1937 in New York City's Harlem. His parents came from Jamaica. Powell attended South Bronx High School and earned a degree in geology from the City College of New York in 1958.

His Calling

Powell says he found his calling when he entered the U.S. military after graduation. He did two tours of duty in Vietnam, in 1962 and 1968. By 1966, Powell had reached the rank of major. During his second tour in Vietnam, he rescued men from a burning helicopter, earning a medal for bravery.

After serving in Vietnam, Powell came to Washington, D.C., where he earned a master's degree in business administration from George Washington University. In 1972, he won a yearlong White House fellowship. Powell was assigned to work in the Office of Management and Budget.

Rising Through the Ranks

In following years, Powell continued his steady rise through the ranks of the military. In 1983, Powell worked as the senior military assistant to Secretary of Defense Caspar Weinberger.

Powell became a lieutenant general in 1986 and took over command of the Fifth U.S. Army Corps in Germany. In 1987, President Ronald Reagan appointed Powell to be his national security adviser. He was the nation's first African American to fill the post.

Top of the Military

In 1989, President George H. W. Bush promoted Powell to the most senior position in the military, chairman of the Joint Chiefs of Staff. Powell was the first African American, and at 52, the youngest officer, to achieve this high honor.

The chairman of the Joint Chiefs of Staff leads the chiefs of staff of the Army, the Navy, the Air Force, and the Marine Corps. Together, they advise the president on military issues. In this role, Colin Powell oversaw many American military operations, including the Persian Gulf War.

After the Military

Powell retired from the military in 1993. There was speculation that he would pursue a political career. Many people expected he would run against Bill Clinton in the 1996 presidential election. Powell did not enter the race. He decided his talents could

be used elsewhere. In 1997, he founded America's Promise, a foundation to help children and youth rise above poverty.

Secretary of State

On January 20, 2001, President George W. Bush appointed Powell the 65th secretary of state. Powell faced many challenges surrounding the terrorist attacks of September 11, 2001. He resigned as secretary of state in 2004.

Colin Powell is one of the most decorated individuals in U.S. history. His numerous awards include two Presidential Medals of Freedom and the Congressional Gold Medal.

Powell led U.S. forces in the Persian Gulf War in 1990 and 1991. He earned the respect of members of the military and the American public.

Secretary Rice

Condoleezza Rice was born in 1954, in Birmingham, Alabama. She was the only daughter of a Presbyterian minister and a science and music teacher. Rice learned the value of hard work and persistence from an early age. She studied piano and dreamed of becoming a concert pianist. In fact, at just 15 years old, Condoleezza performed with the Denver Symphony Orchestra.

Rice entered the University of Denver. Although she did not pursue her first passion of music as a career, she found another in politics. Rice studied international relations as an undergraduate. After graduating in 1974, she earned a doctorate degree in political science.

Professor

Rice began teaching at Stanford University in 1981. She specialized in the Soviet Union, the former country that included Russia and various other republics before it was dissolved in 1991. She met Brent Scowcroft during this time. When Scowcroft became national security adviser in the White House in 1989, he asked Rice to serve as his Soviet expert. Soon, Rice was advising George H. W. Bush on relations with Soviet leader Mikhail Gorbachev.

In 1991, Rice returned to Stanford University. In 1993, Stanford hired her as its provost, or administrative officer. Rice was the university's youngest person, first female, and first African American to serve in this position.

In Government

When George W. Bush ran for president in 2000, he asked Rice to be his foreign policy adviser. Bush went on to win the election and appointed Rice his national security adviser. She worked closely with the president after the September 11, 2001, terrorist attacks on the country. As head of the National Security Council, she took part in major decisions about foreign policy, including the invasion of Iraq.

On January 26, 2005, Condoleezza Rice was sworn in as the 66th secretary of state. She followed Colin Powell in the position. Rice championed a **diplomacy** that involved working with other nations to create sustainable democracy and peace in the world.

Rice was an important adviser to President George W. Bush throughout his two terms.

Quick Facts

Condoleezza is a variation of *con dolcezza*, a musical term that means "with sweetness" in Italian.

Rice remembers the challenges of life in the South for African Americans during the 1960s. She has recalled having to change in a broom closet at a department store in Alabama because she was not permitted to use the changing room.

Rice became a Republican in 1982. She later explained, "My father joined [the Republican Party] because the Democrats in 'Jim Crow' Alabama of 1952 would not register him to vote. The Republicans did."

The 44th U.S. President

Barack Hussein Obama II was born August 4, 1961, in Honolulu, Hawaii. His mother, Ann Dunham, was of European descent. His father, Barack Obama Sr., was from the African country of Kenya. The couple met while attending the University of Hawaii. They divorced in 1964. Barack's father returned to Kenya, and his mother remarried. In 1967, Barack moved with his mother and stepfather to Jakarta, Indonesia. At 10, Barack returned to Honolulu to live with his mother's parents and attend school there.

An Education
After attending Occidental College in Los Angeles, California, Obama moved to New York City. He earned a political science degree from Columbia University in 1983. In 1985, Obama worked as the director of a community organization that helped people in a low-income area of Chicago, Illinois.

In 1988, Obama entered Harvard Law School. He graduated in 1991, and in 1992, he married a lawyer from Chicago named Michelle Robinson. Back in Chicago, he taught at the University of Chicago Law School. He practiced as an attorney, focusing on civil rights cases, and continued his community work.

Public Office
Obama was first elected to public office in 1997 as an Illinois state senator. He supported reforms in education, housing, and workers' rights. Barack Obama gave a speech at the 2004 Democratic **Convention** emphasizing unity and cooperation. The young state senator impressed live and television audiences with his inspiring message and confidence.

Journey to the White House
On February 10, 2007, Obama stood on the steps of the Old State Capitol in Springfield, Illinois, to announce his bid for the presidency. In a hard-fought campaign, Obama won the Democratic nomination over Hillary Clinton, the wife of the former president.

On November 4, 2008, Barack Obama was elected the 44th president of the United States. Obama's historic win was an achievement for all Americans. "If there is anyone out there who still doubts that America is a place where all things are possible," Obama told the world on election night, ". . . tonight is your answer."

As President
When he took office, President Obama faced dramatic challenges. They included the worse financial crisis since the 1930s and two wars, in Afghanistan and Iraq. Obama moved quickly to get legislation enacted to help the struggling economy.

One of Obama's great gifts has always been an ability to communicate. People around the world have responded to his words and vision. In 2009, Obama won the Nobel Peace Prize for his efforts "to strengthen international diplomacy and cooperation."

In law school, Barack Obama was the first African American to serve as president of the famous *Harvard Law Review*.

Marching Forward

The commitment, efforts, and sacrifices of African Americans throughout history have led to many political gains for African Americans, as well as victories in the struggle for equal rights. Work remains to be done, however, and there are still challenges ahead. History has already taught many lessons about the best ways to achieve political change.

Today, groups such as the NAACP and the Congressional Black **Caucus**, or CBC, as well as individuals in many fields, continue to work for the advancement of African Americans and the country as a whole. They believe that education, open discussion, and peaceful protest will help Americans learn more about the issues and one another.

A Historic Achievement

A great political moment in American history took place in the nation's capital on January 20, 2009. Barack Obama took the oath of office as president of the United States. In earlier American history, millions of African Americans were enslaved. As recently as the mid-1900s, segregation was legally enforced in many parts of the country. Even after legal segregation ended, African Americans faced discrimination in American society. Many people expressed the view that, despite their hopes, they did not think they would live to see the day that an African American would be sworn in as president. The fact that such a day did come is a symbol of the gains African Americans have achieved in American politics and American life.

The CBC

Organizations such as the Congressional Black Caucus reflect some of the political power and influence of African Americans today. The CBC is an organization of African American members of Congress. It was founded in 1971 to promote the goals of African American and other minority citizens. The group has focused on issues such as voting rights, health care, and employment. As of 2011, the CBC has 43 members.

Timeline

1619: Africans are captured and brought to Jamestown, Virginia, to work as slaves.

1641: Mathias de Sousa may have been the first African American elected to a legislative body in what is now the United States.

1845: Frederick Douglass publishes an autobiography called *Narrative of the Life of Frederick Douglass, an American Slave.*

1845

1857: The Supreme Court rules that African Americans, free or enslaved, are not considered U.S. citizens.

1863

1863: President Abraham Lincoln issues the Emancipation Proclamation, which frees slaves in Confederate areas.

1865: The 13th Amendment to the U.S. Constitution officially abolishes slavery.

1870: Hiram Rhodes Revels becomes the first African American elected to the U.S. Senate.

1875: The U.S. Congress enacts the Civil Rights Act of 1875, guaranteeing equal rights to African Americans. It is declared unconstitutional in 1883.

1877: Reconstruction ends with the withdrawal of federal troops from the Southern states by President Rutherford Hayes.

1881: On July 4, Booker T. Washington opens the school that is now Tuskegee University, focused on the education of African Americans.

1895: W. E. B. Du Bois becomes the first African American to earn a doctorate degree from Harvard University.

1895

1909: The National Association for the Advancement of Colored People, or NAACP, is founded in New York City.

1913: After leading hundreds of slaves to freedom in the North, Harriet Tubman dies.

1913

1600   **1850**   **1870**   **1900**

1942: The Congress of Racial Equality, or CORE, is founded in Chicago.

1957: Martin Luther King Jr. forms the Southern Christian Leadership Conference.

1964: President Lyndon B. Johnson signs the Civil Rights Act of 1964 in Washington, D.C.

1965: Malcolm X is shot and killed in New York.

1984

1991: In Washington, D.C., Sharon Pratt Kelly becomes the first African American woman to serve as mayor of a major American city.

1992: Carol Moseley Braun is the first African American woman elected to the U.S. Senate.

1965

1984: Jesse Jackson makes his first bid for the Democratic nomination for president of the United States.

1989: Ronald H. Brown, elected chair of the Democratic National Committee, is the first African American to head a major political party.

2009

1966

1966: The Black Panther Party is founded in Oakland, California.

1968: Shirley Chisholm becomes the first African American woman to be elected to Congress.

1973: Thomas Bradley becomes the first African American mayor of Los Angeles.

1968

2009: Barack Obama becomes the 44th U.S. president and the first African American president.

1940   1960   1980   2010

Activity

What Makes a Political Leader?

A leader is someone whom others consider a role model. Leaders have shaped our world. In this activity, you will examine what makes a political leader.

First, define the word *leader* in your own words. What characteristics do leaders have? Next, look up the word *leader* in a dictionary. Compare that definition to your own. What traits on your list are the same as or different from the dictionary definition?

Now, think about who your personal leaders are. They might be a parent, a grandparent, a teacher, a neighbor, or a famous person. Write a short paragraph about this person and why you look up to this person.

Finally, consider some of the great leaders of African American politics. Choose one, and write a short biography of his or her life. Use reliable sites on the Internet to help you research the details. What was his or her impact, and what made him or her a great political leader?

You will need:

✓ a pen
✓ paper
✓ a dictionary
✓ access to the Internet

Test Your Knowledge

Q Who led hundreds of escaped slaves from the South to freedom in northern states or in Canada on the Underground Railroad?

A Harriet Tubman

Q Who was the first African American to serve in the U.S. Senate?

A Hiram Rhodes Revels

Q What year did the United States abolish slavery?

A 1865

Q What was the name given to the local and state laws that required segregation of African Americans?

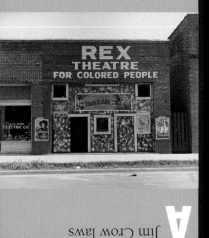

A Jim Crow laws

Q Who was the first African American appointed to the U.S. Supreme Court?

A Thurgood Marshall

Q What does CBC stand for?

A Congressional Black Caucus

Glossary

activist: a person who acts to bring about change for a cause

amendment: a change to a law or constitution

bail: a fine paid to temporarily release a person from jail

boycott: the action of refusing to use a public service or purchase goods and services

caucus: a group of people who support a political party or movement

citizens: members of a country or political community

civil rights: the basic rights guaranteed to the citizens of a country

Civil War: a war that took place in the United States between 1861 and 1865 in which states in the North fought the states in the South that had seceded, or left, the Union

Congress: the national lawmaking body of a nation; the U.S. Congress is made up of the Senate and the House of Representatives

convention: a formal gathering of a group

Democratic Party: one of the two main U.S. political parties

diplomacy: the skill or practice of conducting international relations

discrimination: unfair treatment due to prejudice

doctorate degree: the highest degree awarded by a university

Emancipation Proclamation: an official announcement issued by President Abraham Lincoln in 1863 freeing slaves in the Confederate states

federal: relating to the national branch of government

infantry: the army branch made up of soldiers trained to fight on foot

Islam: a religion founded by an Arab religious leader named Muhammad

Jim Crow laws: laws that supported segregation in the Southern states

Ku Klux Klan: a terrorist group that uses violence against minority groups

legislative: having to do with lawmaking

race riot: a violent outbreak that is caused by racial hatred or disagreement

racist: someone who discriminates based on a person's race

Reconstruction: the time between 1865 and 1877 when Southern states tried to rebuild and adapt to the laws of the United States

Republican Party: one of the two main U.S. political parties

segregation: a forced separation of races

sit-ins: organized demonstrations in which protesters sit in one spot and refuse to move

terrorist: a person who uses extreme acts to frighten others

unconstitutional: not in agreement with the U.S. Constitution, which sets out the rights and freedoms of all Americans

Underground Railroad: a network of people, safe houses, and resources used to help African Americans escape slavery

U.S. Supreme Court: the highest court in the United States

World War II: a global conflict fought from 1939 to 1945

Index

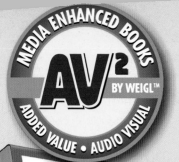

Log on to www.av2books.com

AV² by Weigl brings you media enhanced books that support active learning. Go to www.av2books.com, and enter the special code found on page 2 of this book. You will gain access to enriched and enhanced content that supplements and complements this book. Content includes video, audio, web links, quizzes, a slide show, and activities.

Audio
Listen to sections of the book read aloud.

Video
Watch informative video clips.

Embedded Weblinks
Gain additional information for research.

Try This!
Complete activities and hands-on experiments.

WHAT'S ONLINE?

Try This!	Embedded Weblinks	Video	EXTRA FEATURES
Test your knowledge of important events in African American political history.	Find out more about the history of African Americans in politics.	Watch a video about African Americans in politics.	**Audio** Listen to sections of the book read aloud.
Write a biography about a notable African American politician.	Learn more about notable people from **Great African Americans Politics**.	Watch a video about a notable moment of African Americans in politics.	**Key Words** Study vocabulary, and complete a matching word activity.
Create a timeline of important events in an African American politician's life.	Link to more notable achievements of African Americans in politics.		**Slide Show** View images and captions, and prepare a presentation.
Complete a writing activity about an important topic in the book.			**Quizzes** Test your knowledge.
Outline an important political movement.			

AV² was built to bridge the gap between print and digital. We encourage you to tell us what you like and what you want to see in the future.

Sign up to be an AV² Ambassador at www.av2books.com/ambassador.